Revolution and Romanticism, 1789-1834

A series of facsimile reprints chosen and introduced by
Jonathan Wordsworth
University Lecturer in Romantic Studies at Oxford

Coleridge
Christabel 1816

Samuel Taylor Coleridge

Christabel
1816

Woodstock Books
Oxford and New York
1991

This edition first published 1991 by
Woodstock Books
Spelsbury House, Spelsbury, Oxford OX7 3JR
and
Woodstock Books
Wordsworth Trust America
Department of English, City College
Convent Ave and 138th St, New York, N.Y. 10031

British Library Cataloguing in Publication Data
Coleridge, Samuel Taylor, 1772-1834
  Christabel 1816. – (Revolution and romanticism, 1789-
  1834)
  I. Title   II. Series
  821.6
  ISBN 1-85477-063-2

Printed and bound in Great Britain by
Smith Settle
Otley, West Yorkshire LS21 3JP

Introduction

'Coleridge', Lamb wrote to Wordsworth in a delightful letter of 26 April 1816:

is printing *Xtabel* by Ld Byron's recommendation to Murray, with what he calls a vision, *Kubla Khan* – which said vision he repeats so enchantingly that it irradiates and brings heaven and Elysian bowers into my parlour while he sings or says it.

The thought of Coleridge chanting *Kubla Khan* in the parlour has a marvellous and magical incongruity:

> Weave a circle round him thrice,
> And close your eyes with holy dread:
> For he on honey-dew hath fed,
> And drunk the milk of Paradise.

Lamb was the ideal audience, but knew enough of the ways of reviewers to fear for the poem when it was brought to light:

there is an observation, Never tell thy dreams, and I am almost afraid that *Kubla Khan* is an owl that won't bear day light; I fear lest it should be discovered by the lantern of typography . . . no better than nonsense or no sense.

Lamb was not wrong, but *Christabel*, when it came to the point, was received with quite as much incomprehension. Not all the reviews were hostile. The *Critical*, for instance, retells the story in May 1816 with sympathy, concluding that *Christabel* is a 'very graceful and fanciful poem . . . enriched with more beautiful passages than have ever been before included in so small a compass.' More typical, however, are the tones of the *British review* ('We really must make a stand somewhere for the rights of common sense') and the pompous *Anti-jacobin*: 'gravely to discuss so wretched a performance is beneath the dignity of criticism'. An essay in the *Edinburgh* regards the whole volume 'as one of the most notable pieces of impertinence of which the press has lately been guilty'. It is 'utterly destitute of value'. The reviewer (commonly thought to be Moore) is prepared to 'defy any man to point out a passage of poetical merit in any of the three pieces which [the book] contains'.

Moore's friend, Byron, would certainly have accepted the challenge. On 18 October 1815 he had written to Coleridge:

[Scott] repeated to me a considerable portion of an unpublished poem of yours – the wildest and finest I ever heard in that kind of composition – the title he did not mention – but I think the heroine's name was Geraldine . . . [it] took a hold of my imagination that I never shall wish to shake off.

The tones recall Lamb's comment to Wordsworth on the *Ancient mariner* in January 1801: 'I was never so affected with any human Tale. After first reading it, I was totally possessed with it for many days'. Byron's purpose, however, was to ask whether the two completed sections of *Christabel* (Part I, 1798, Part II, 1800) were to be included in *Sybilline leaves* (printed 1815, published two years later). Learning that they weren't, he at first urged Coleridge to complete the poem, then arranged with Murray to publish it as it stood. Six months later, in April 1816, *Christabel* was in print, sharing a slim octavo with *Kubla Khan* and the beautiful, yet terrible, *Pains of sleep*.

No answer has been preserved to Byron's letter of October 1815. Coleridge was probably too deferent to remark the lapse of memory that made Geraldine hero of *Christabel* (and her creator 'a member of the devil's party'), but he seems to have had strong words to say about Scott's plagiarism in the *Lay of the last minstrel*. Answering Coleridge's complaints on 27 October, Byron is tactful and judicious: 'though I cannot contradict your statement . . . all I have ever seen of [Scott] has been frank – fair and warm in regards to you'. Scott had memorized parts of *Christabel* as early as 1802, when it was repeated to him in Edinburgh by Coleridge's friend (and Hazlitt's future brother-in-law), John Stoddart. The effect on the *Minstrel* (1805) is there for all to see. Critics might grumble that *Christabel* was unfinished and unintelligible, but Coleridge's fellow poets had no doubts as to its power. Wordsworth drew on it in the *Waggoner* and *White doe of Rylstone*, Scott in the *Minstrel*, Keats in *Eve of St Agnes* and *Lamia*; Byron, meanwhile, found himself telling Coleridge that similarities between *The siege of Corinth* and *Christabel* were merely chance. Perhaps they were. But Coleridge's poem, with its strange metre and strange supernatural goings-on, was quietly pervasive.

Lamb's views of *Kubla Khan* are echoed, in a rather less generous tone of voice, by Hazlitt in the *Examiner* of 2 June 1816:

Kubla Khan, we think, only shews that Mr Coleridge can write better *nonsense* verses than any man in England. It is not a poem, but a musical composition.

    A damsel with a dulcimer
    In a vision once I saw:
    It was an Abyssianian maid,
    And on her dulcimer she play'd,
    Singing of Mount Abora.

'We could repeat these lines to ourselves', Hazlitt adds ungraciously, 'not the less often for not knowing the meaning of them'. Meaning is a preoccupation with the reviewers. By presenting *Kubla Khan* as a vision and 'a psychological curiosity', Coleridge has disclaimed responsibility for its content. Josiah Conder in the *Eclectic review* (June 1816) is especially indignant: 'We could have informed Mr Coleridge of a reverend friend of ours, who actually wrote down two sermons on a passage in the Apocalypse, from the recollection of the spontaneous exercise of his faculties in sleep.'

Christabel (though it did at least tell a story) was again deliberately enigmatic. Hazlitt, who saw it gruesomely as containing 'something disgusting at the bottom . . . like moon-beams playing on a charnel-house, or flowers strewed on a dead body', was exercised that Coleridge should have left out of the printed text a line in the manuscript describing Geraldine's side and bosom as 'lean and old and foul of hue'. The line, he asserts, is necessary to make common sense . . . 'It is the key-stone that makes up the arch'. For that reason Mr Coleridge left it out.

On both counts Hazlitt is right, but he must have been surprised to find himself siding with the *British review* as the champion of common sense. Disapproval of Coleridge's politics has been allowed too obviously to affect his critical judgment. Mystery is essential to poetry, doubly so to poetry of the supernatural. Geraldine's nakedness must remain 'A sight to dream of, not to tell', just as the war prophesied by 'ancestral voices' in *Kubla Khan* must forever remain enigmatic. As it happens, the enigma of *Christabel* is at its most pronounced in the text of 1816. Not only has Coleridge cut the one gratuitously informative line, he has yet to insert the passage that offers his clearest hints as to Geraldine's nature – possessed, surely, rather than evil:

> Yet Geraldine nor speaks nor stirs;
> Ah! what a stricken look was hers!
> Deep from within she seems half-way
> To lift some weight with sick assay,
> And eyes the maid and seeks delay;
> Then suddenly, as one defied,
> Collects herself in scorn and pride,
> And lay down by the Maiden's side . . .

Printed on its own alongside two of Coleridge's three masterpieces, *Pains of sleep* (1803) might seem a little exposed. Where *Christabel* and *Kubla Khan* have individual prefaces (the second so compelling in its myth of inspiration and interruption as to be inseparable from the poem ever after), *Pains of sleep* has a single sentence:

> As a contrast to this vision [*Kubla Khan*], I have annexed a fragment of a very different character, describing with equal fidelity the dream of pain and disease.

As with *Kubla Khan*, the word 'fragment' is used as a kind of self-deprecation, an attempt to ward off criticism. *Pains of sleep* (1803) is beautifully rounded, a perfect whole. Once again, however, it is a kind of poetry for which the critics had no precedent. Coleridge, in what is almost the last of his great poems, has found a way to express in personal terms the horrors, yearnings, guilt and confusion, that we sense in the *Ancient mariner*. The poem is not a fragment, and not a dream, and is by no means solely concerned with 'pain and disease', but it does have a marvellous fidelity. This is what it was like to experience the nightmare alternations in mood of Coleridge's opium years:

> Ere on my bed my limbs I lay,
> It hath not been my use to pray
> With moving lips or bended knees;
> But silently, by slow degrees,
> My spirit I to Love compose . . .
> But yester-night I pray'd aloud
> In anguish and in agony,
> Upstarting from the fiendish crowd
> Of shapes and thoughts that tortured me . . .
> Such punishments, I said, were due
> To natures deepliest stain'd with sin:
> For aye entempesting anew
> Th'unfathomable hell within
> The horror of their deeds to view,
> To know and loathe, yet wish and do!
> Such griefs with such men well agree,
> But wherefore, wherefore fall on me?
> To be beloved is all I need,
> And whom I love, I love indeed.

J W

Christabel, &c.

CHRISTABEL:

KUBLA KHAN,

A VISION;

THE PAINS OF SLEEP.

BY

S. T. COLERIDGE, ESQ.

LONDON:

PRINTED FOR JOHN MURRAY, ALBEMARLE-STREET,

BY WILLIAM BULMER AND CO. CLEVELAND-ROW,

ST. JAMES'S.

1816.

PREFACE.

———

THE first part of the following poem was written in the year one thousand seven hundred and ninety seven, at Stowey in the county of Somerset. The second part, after my return from Germany, in the year one thousand eight hundred, at Keswick, Cumberland. Since the latter date, my poetic powers have been, till very lately, in a state of suspended animation. But as, in my very first conception of the tale, I had the whole present to my mind, with the wholeness, no less than with the liveliness of a vision; I trust that I shall be able to embody in verse the three parts yet to come, in the course of the present year.

It is probable, that if the poem had been finished at either of the former periods, or if even the first and second part had been published in the year 1800, the impression of its originality would have been much greater than I dare at present expect. But for this, I have only my own indolence to blame. The dates are mentioned for the exclusive purpose of precluding charges of plagiarism or servile imitation from myself. For there is among us a set of critics, who seem to hold, that every possible thought and image is traditional; who have no notion that there are such things as fountains in the world, small as well as great; and who would therefore charitably derive every rill, they behold flowing, from a perforation made in some other man's tank. I am confident however, that as far as the present poem is concerned, the celebrated poets whose writings I might be suspected of having imitated, either in particular passages, or

in the tone and the spirit of the whole, would be
among the first to vindicate me from the charge,
and who, on any striking coincidence, would
permit me to address them in this doggrel version
of two monkish Latin hexameters:

> 'Tis mine and it is likewise your's,
> But an if this will not do;
> Let it be mine, good friend! for I
> Am the poorer of the two.

I have only to add, that the metre of the
Christabel is not, properly speaking, irregular,
though it may seem so from its being founded
on a new principle: namely, that of counting in
each line the accents, not the syllables. Though
the latter may vary from seven to twelve, yet in
each line the accents will be found to be only
four. Nevertheless this occasional variation in
the number of syllables is not introduced wan-
tonly, or for the mere ends of convenience, but
in correspondence with some transition in the
nature of the imagery or passion.

CHRISTABEL.

PART I.

CHRISTABEL.

'Tis the middle of night by the castle clock,
And the owls have awaken'd the crowing cock;
Tu—whit!———Tu—whoo!
And hark, again! the crowing cock,
How drowsily it crew.

Sir Leoline, the Baron rich,
Hath a toothless mastiff bitch;

From her kennel beneath the rock
She makes answer to the clock,
Four for the quarters, and twelve for the hour ;
Ever and aye, moonshine or shower,
Sixteen short howls, not over loud ;
Some say, she sees my lady's shroud.

Is the night chilly and dark ?
The night is chilly, but not dark.
The thin gray cloud is spread on high,
It covers but not hides the sky.
The moon is behind, and at the full ;
And yet she looks both small and dull.
The night is chill, the cloud is gray :
'Tis a month before the month of May,
And the Spring comes slowly up this way.

The lovely lady, Christabel,
Whom her father loves so well,

What makes her in the wood so late,
A furlong from the castle gate?
She had dreams all yesternight
Of her own betrothed knight;
Dreams, that made her moan and leap,
As on her bed she lay in sleep;
And she in the midnight wood will pray
For the weal of her lover that's far away.

She stole along, she nothing spoke,
The breezes they were still also;
And nought was green upon the oak,
But moss and rarest misletoe:
She kneels beneath the huge oak tree,
And in silence prayeth she.

The lady leaps up suddenly,
The lovely lady, Christabel!

It moan'd as near, as near can be,
But what it is, she cannot tell.—
On the other side it seems to be,
Of the huge, broad-breasted, old oak tree.

The night is chill; the forest bare;
Is it the wind that moaneth bleak?
There is not wind enough in the air
To move away the ringlet curl
From the lovely lady's cheek —
There is not wind enough to twirl
The one red leaf, the last of its clan,
That dances as often as dance it can,
Hanging so light, and hanging so high,
On the topmost twig that looks up at the sky.

Hush, beating heart of Christabel!
Jesu, Maria, shield her well!

She folded her arms beneath her cloak,
And stole to the other side of the oak.
What sees she there?

There she sees a damsel bright,
Drest in a silken robe of white;
Her neck, her feet, her arms were bare,
And the jewels disorder'd in her hair.
I guess, 'twas frightful there to see
A lady so richly clad as she—
Beautiful exceedingly!

Mary mother, save me now!
(Said Christabel,) And who art thou?

The lady strange made answer meet,
And her voice was faint and sweet:—
Have pity on my sore distress,
I scarce can speak for weariness.

Stretch forth thy hand, and have no fear,
Said Christabel, How cam'st thou here?
And the lady, whose voice was faint and sweet,
Did thus pursue her answer meet :—

My sire is of a noble line,
And my name is Geraldine.
Five warriors seiz'd me yestermorn,
Me, even me, a maid forlorn :
They chok'd my cries with force and fright,
And tied me on a palfrey white.
The palfrey was as fleet as wind,
And they rode furiously behind.
They spurr'd amain, their steeds were white ;
And once we cross'd the shade of night.
As sure as Heaven shall rescue me,
I have no thought what men they be ;
Nor do I know how long it is
(For I have lain in fits, I wis)

Since one, the tallest of the five,

Took me from the palfrey's back,

A weary woman, scarce alive.

Some mutter'd words his comrades spoke :

He plac'd me underneath this oak,

He swore they would return with haste ;

Whither they went I cannot tell —

I thought I heard, some minutes past,

Sounds as of a castle bell.

Stretch forth thy hand (thus ended she),

And help a wretched maid to flee.

Then Christabel stretch'd forth her hand

And comforted fair Geraldine,

Saying, that she should command

The service of Sir Leoline ;

And straight be convoy'd, free from thrall,

Back to her noble father's hall.

So up she rose, and forth they pass'd,
With hurrying steps, yet nothing fast ;
Her lucky stars the lady blest,
And Christabel she sweetly said—
All our household are at rest,
Each one sleeping in his bed ;
Sir Leoline is weak in health,
And may not well awaken'd be ;
So to my room we'll creep in stealth,
And you to-night must sleep with me.

They cross'd the moat, and Christabel
Took the key that fitted well ;
A little door she open'd straight,
All in the middle of the gate ;
The gate that was iron'd within and without,
Where an army in battle array had march'd out.

The lady sank, belike thro' pain,
And Christabel with might and main
Lifted her up, a weary weight,
Over the threshold of the gate:
Then the lady rose again,
And mov'd, as she were not in pain.

So free from danger, free from fear,
They cross'd the court : right glad they were.
And Christabel devoutly cried,
To the lady by her side,
Praise we the Virgin all divine
Who hath rescued thee from thy distress!
Alas, alas! said Geraldine,
I cannot speak for weariness.
So free from danger, free from fear,
They cross'd the court : right glad they were

Outside her kennel, the mastiff old
Lay fast asleep, in moonshine cold.
The mastiff old did not awake,
Yet she an angry moan did make !
And what can ail the mastiff bitch ?
Never till now she utter'd yell
Beneath the eye of Christabel.
Perhaps it is the owlet's scritch:
For what can ail the mastiff bitch ?

They pass'd the hall, that echoes still,
Pass as lightly as you will !
The brands were flat, the brands were dying,
Amid their own white ashes lying ;
But when the lady pass'd, there came
A tongue of light, a fit of flame ;
And Christabel saw the lady's eye,
And nothing else saw she thereby,

Save the boss of the shield of Sir Leoline tall,
Which hung in a murky old nitch in the wall.
O softly tread, said Christabel,
My father seldom sleepeth well.

Sweet Christabel her feet she bares,
And they are creeping up the stairs ;
Now in glimmer, and now in gloom,
And now they pass the Baron's room,
As still as death with stifled breath !
And now have reach'd her chamber door ;
And now with eager feet press down
The rushes of her chamber floor.

The moon shines dim in the open air,
And not a moonbeam enters here.
But they without its light can see
The chamber carv'd so curiously,

Carv'd with figures strange and sweet,
All made out of the carver's brain,
For a lady's chamber meet :
The lamp with twofold silver chain
Is fasten'd to an angel's feet.

The silver lamp burns dead and dim ;
But Christabel the lamp will trim.
She trimm'd the lamp, and made it bright,
And left it swinging to and fro,
While Geraldine, in wretched plight,
Sank down upon the floor below.

O weary lady, Geraldine,
I pray you, drink this cordial wine !
It is a wine of virtuous powers ;
My mother made it of wild flowers.

And will your mother pity me,
Who am a maiden most forlorn ?

Christabel answer'd—Woe is me!
She died the hour that I was born.
I have heard the gray-hair'd friar tell,
How on her death-bed she did say,
That she should hear the castle bell
Strike twelve upon my wedding day.
O mother dear! that thou wert here!
I would, said Geraldine, she were!

But soon with alter'd voice, said she—
" Off, wandering mother! Peak and pine !
" I have power to bid thee flee."
Alas! what ails poor Geraldine ?
Why stares she with unsettled eye ?
Can she the bodiless dead espy ?
And why with hollow voice cries she,
" Off, woman, off! this hour is mine —
" Though thou her guardian spirit be,
" Off, woman, off! 'tis given to me."

Then Christabel knelt by the lady's side,
And rais'd to heaven her eyes so blue—
Alas! said she, this ghastly ride—
Dear lady! it hath wilder'd you!
The lady wip'd her moist cold brow,
And faintly said, " 'Tis over now !"

Again the wild-flower wine she drank :
Her fair large eyes 'gan glitter bright,
And from the floor whereon she sank,
The lofty lady stood upright :
She was most beautiful to see,
Like a lady of a far countrée.

And thus the lofty lady spake —
All they, who live in the upper sky,
Do love you, holy Christabel !
And you love them, and for their sake
And for the good which me befel,

Even I in my degree will try,
Fair maiden, to requite you well.
But now unrobe yourself; for I
Must pray, ere yet in bed I lie.

Quoth Christabel, so let it be!
And as the lady bade, did she.
Her gentle limbs did she undress,
And lay down in her loveliness.

But thro' her brain of weal and woe
So many thoughts mov'd to and fro,
That vain it were her lids to close;
So half-way from the bed she rose,
And on her elbow did recline
To look at the lady Geraldine.

Beneath the lamp the lady bow'd,
And slowly roll'd her eyes around;

Then drawing in her breath aloud,
Like one that shudder'd, she unbound
The cincture from beneath her breast:
Her silken robe, and inner vest,
Dropt to her feet, and full in view,
Behold! her bosom and half her side——
A sight to dream of, not to tell!
And she is to sleep by Christabel.

She took two paces, and a stride,
And lay down by the maiden's side:
And in her arms the maid she took,
                Ah wel-a-day!
And with low voice and doleful look
These words did say:
In the touch of this bosom there worketh a spell,
Which is lord of thy utterance, Christabel!
Thou knowest to-night, and wilt know to-morrow
This mark of my shame, this seal of my sorrow;

But vainly thou warrest,
   For this is alone in
Thy power to declare,
   That in the dim forest
   Thou heard'st a low moaning,
And found'st a bright lady, surpassingly fair :
And didst bring her home with thee in love and in
   charity,
To shield her and shelter her from the damp air.

THE CONCLUSION

TO

PART THE FIRST.

It was a lovely sight to see
The lady Christabel, when she
Was praying at the old oak tree.

    Amid the jagged shadows
    Of mossy leafless boughs,
    Kneeling in the moonlight,
    To make her gentle vows ;
Her slender palms together prest,
Heaving sometimes on her breast ;
Her face resign'd to bliss or bale—
Her face, oh call it fair not pale,

And both blue eyes more bright than clear,
Each about to have a tear.

With open eyes (ah woe is me!)
Asleep, and dreaming fearfully,
Fearfully dreaming, yet I wis,
Dreaming that alone, which is——
O sorrow and shame! Can this be she,
The lady, who knelt at the old oak tree?
And lo! the worker of these harms,
That holds the maiden in her arms,
Seems to slumber still and mild,
As a mother with her child.

A star hath set, a star hath risen,
O Geraldine! since arms of thine
Have been the lovely lady's prison.
O Geraldine! one hour was thine—

Thou'st had thy will! By tairn and rill,
The night-birds all that hour were still.
But now they are jubilant anew,
From cliff and tower, tu—whoo! tu—whoo!
Tu—whoo! tu—whoo! from wood and fell!

And see! the lady Christabel
Gathers herself from out her trance;
Her limbs relax, her countenance
Grows sad and soft; the smooth thin lids
Close o'er her eyes; and tears she sheds—
Large tears that leave the lashes bright!
And oft the while she seems to smile
As infants at a sudden light!

Yea, she doth smile, and she doth weep,
Like a youthful hermitess,
Beauteous in a wilderness,
Who, praying always, prays in sleep.

And, if she move unquietly,

Perchance, 'tis but the blood so free,

Comes back and tingles in her feet.

No doubt, she hath a vision sweet.

What if her guardian spirit 'twere

What if she knew her mother near?

But this she knows, in joys and woes,

That saints will aid if men will call:

For the blue sky bends over all!

CHRISTABEL.

PART II.

CHRISTABEL.

———

Each matin bell, the Baron saith,
Knells us back to a world of death.
These words Sir Leoline first said,
When he rose and found his lady dead :
These words Sir Leoline will say
Many a morn to his dying day.

And hence the custom and law began,
That still at dawn the sacristan,
Who duly pulls the heavy bell,
Five and forty beads must tell
Between each stroke—a warning knell,
Which not a soul can choose but hear
From Bratha Head to Wyn'dermere.

Saith Bracy the bard, So let it knell!
And let the drowsy sacristan
Still count as slowly as he can!
There is no lack of such, I ween
As well fill up the space between.
In Langdale Pike and Witch's Lair,
And Dungeon-ghyll so foully rent,
With ropes of rock and bells of air
Three sinful sextons' ghosts are pent,
Who all give back, one after t'other,
The death-note to their living brother;

And oft too, by the knell offended,
Just as their one! two! three! is ended,
The devil mocks the doleful tale
With a merry peal from Borrowdale.

The air is still! thro' mist and cloud
That merry peal comes ringing loud;
And Geraldine shakes off her dread,
And rises lightly from the bed;
Puts on her silken vestments white,
And tricks her hair in lovely plight,
And nothing doubting of her spell
Awakens the lady Christabel.
" Sleep you, sweet lady Christabel?
" I trust that you have rested well."

And Christabel awoke and spied
The same who lay down by her side—

O rather say, the same whom she
Rais'd up beneath the old oak tree !
Nay, fairer yet ! and yet more fair !
For she belike hath drunken deep
Of all the blessedness of sleep !
And while she spake, her looks, her air
Such gentle thankfulness declare,
That (so it seem'd) her girded vests
Grew tight beneath her heaving breasts.
" Sure I have sinn'd !" said Christabel,
" Now heaven be prais'd if all be well !"
And in low faltering tones, yet sweet,
Did she the lofty lady greet
With such perplexity of mind
As dreams too lively leave behind.

So quickly she rose, and quickly array'd
Her maiden limbs, and having pray'd

That He, who on the cross did groan,
Might wash away her sins unknown,
She forthwith led fair Geraldine
To meet her sire, Sir Leoline.

The lovely maid and the lady tall
Are pacing both into the hall,
And pacing on thro' page and groom
Enter the Baron's presence room.

The Baron rose, and while he prest
His gentle daughter to his breast,
With cheerful wonder in his eyes
The lady Geraldine espies,
And gave such welcome to the same,
As might beseem so bright a dame!

But when he heard the lady's tale,
And when she told her father's name,

Why wax'd Sir Leoline so pale,
Murmuring o'er the name again,
Lord Roland de Vaux of Tryermaine?

Alas! they had been friends in youth;
But whispering tongues can poison truth;
And constancy lives in realms above;
And life is thorny; and youth is vain;
And to be wroth with one we love,
Doth work like madness in the brain.
And thus it chanc'd, as I divine,
With Roland and Sir Leoline.
Each spake words of high disdain
And insult to his heart's best brother:
They parted—ne'er to meet again!
But never either found another
To free the hollow heart from paining—
They stood aloof, the scars remaining,
Like cliffs which had been rent asunder;

A dreary sea now flows between,
But neither heat, nor frost, nor thunder,
Shall wholly do away, I ween,
The marks of that which once hath been.

Sir Leoline, a moment's space,
Stood gazing on the damsel's face;
And the youthful Lord of Tryermaine
Came back upon his heart again.

O then the Baron forgot his age,
His noble heart swell'd high with rage;
He swore by the wounds in Jesu's side,
He would proclaim it far and wide
With trump and solemn heraldry,
That they, who thus had wrong'd the dame,
Were base as spotted infamy!
" And if they dare deny the same,

D

" My herald shall appoint a week,

" And let the recreant traitors seek

" My tournay court—that there and then

" I may dislodge their reptile souls

" From the bodies and forms of men !"

He spake : his eye in lightning rolls !

For the lady was ruthlessly seiz'd ; and he kenn'd

In the beautiful lady the child of his friend !

And now the tears were on his face,

And fondly in his arms he took

Fair Geraldine, who met th' embrace,

Prolonging it with joyous look.

Which when she view'd, a vision fell

Upon the soul of Christabel,

The vision of fear, the touch and pain !

She shrunk and shudder'd, and saw again

(Ah, woe is me ! Was it for thee,

Thou gentle maid ! such sights to see ?)

Again she saw that bosom old,
Again she felt that bosom cold,
And drew in her breath with a hissing sound :
Whereat the Knight turn'd wildly round,
And nothing saw, but his own sweet maid
With eyes uprais'd, as one that pray'd.

The touch, the sight, had pass'd away,
And in its stead that vision blest,
Which comforted her after-rest,
While in the lady's arms she lay,
Had put a rapture in her breast,
And on her lips and o'er her eyes
Spread smiles like light!
                    With new surprise,
" What ails then my beloved child?"
The Baron said—His daughter mild
Made answer, " All will yet be well!"
I ween, she had no power to tell

Aught else : so mighty was the spell.
Yet he, who saw this Geraldine,
Had deem'd her sure a thing divine,
Such sorrow with such grace she blended,
As if she fear'd, she had offended
Sweet Christabel, that gentle maid !
And with such lowly tones she pray'd,
She might be sent without delay
Home to her father's mansion.

                    " Nay !

" Nay, by my soul !" said Leoline.
'' Ho ! Bracy the bard, the charge be thine !
" Go thou, with music sweet and loud,
" And take two steeds with trappings proud,
" And take the youth whom thou lov'st best
" To bear thy harp, and learn thy song,
" And clothe you both in solemn vest,
" And over the mountains haste along,

" Lest wand'ring folk, that are abroad,

" Detain you on the valley road.

" And when he has cross'd the Irthing flood,

" My merry bard! he hastes, he hastes

" Up Knorren Moor, thro' Halegarth Wood,

" And reaches soon that castle good

" Which stands and threatens Scotland's wastes.

" Bard Bracy! bard Bracy! your horses are fleet,

" Ye must ride up the hall, your music so sweet,

" More loud than your horses' echoing feet!

" And loud and loud to Lord Roland call,

" Thy daughter is safe in Langdale hall !

" Thy beautiful daughter is safe and free—

" Sir Leoline greets thee thus thro' me.

" He bids thee come without delay

" With all thy numerous array ;

" And take thy lovely daughter home,

" And he will meet thee on the way

" With all his numerous array

" White with their panting palfreys' foam,

" And, by mine honour ! I will say,

" That I repent me of the day

" When I spake words of fierce disdain

" To Roland de Vaux of Tryermaine !—

" —For since that evil hour hath flown,

" Many a summer's sun have shone ;

" Yet ne'er found I a friend again

" Like Roland de Vaux of Tryermaine."

The lady fell, and clasped his knees,

Her face uprais'd, her eyes o'erflowing ;

And Bracy replied, with faltering voice,

His gracious hail on all bestowing :—

Thy words, thou sire of Christabel,

Are sweeter than my harp can tell ;

Yet might I gain a boon of thee,

This day my journey should not be,

So strange a dream hath come to me :

That I had vow'd with music loud

To clear yon wood from thing unblest,

Warn'd by a vision in my rest !

For in my sleep I saw that dove,

That gentle bird, whom thou dost love,

And call'st by thy own daughter's name—

Sir Leoline ! I saw the same,

Fluttering, and uttering fearful moan,

Among the green herbs in the forest alone.

Which when I saw and when I heard,

I wonder'd what might ail the bird :

For nothing near it could I see,

Save the grass and green herbs underneath the
old tree.

And in my dream, methought, I went

To search out what might there be found ;

And what the sweet bird's trouble meant,

That thus lay fluttering on the ground.

I went and peer'd, and could descry

No cause for her distressful cry;

But yet for her dear lady's sake

I stoop'd, methought the dove to take,

When lo! I saw a bright green snake

Coil'd around its wings and neck.

Green as the herbs on which it couch'd,

Close by the dove's its head it crouch'd;

And with the dove it heaves and stirs,

Swelling its neck as she swell'd hers!

I woke; it was the midnight hour,

The clock was echoing in the tower;

But tho' my slumber was gone by,

This dream it would not pass away—

It seems to live upon my eye!

And thence I vow'd this self-same day,

With music strong and saintly song

To wander thro' the forest bare,
Lest aught unholy loiter there.

Thus Bracy said : the Baron, the while,
Half-listening heard him with a smile ;
Then turn'd to Lady Geraldine,
His eyes made up of wonder and love ;
And said in courtly accents fine,
Sweet maid, Lord Roland's beauteous dove,
With arms more strong than harp or song,
Thy sire and I will crush the snake !
He kiss'd her forehead as he spake,
And Geraldine in maiden wise,
Casting down her large bright eyes,
With blushing cheek and courtesy fine
She turn'd her from Sir Leoline ;
Softly gathering up her train,
That o'er her right arm fell again ;
And folded her arms across her chest,
And couch'd her head upon her breast,

And look'd askance at Christabel——
Jesu, Maria, shield her well !

A snake's small eye blinks dull and shy,
And the lady's eyes they shrunk in her head,
Each shrunk up to a serpent's eye,
And with somewhat of malice, and more of dread
At Christabel she look'd askance !——
One moment—and the sight was fled !
But Christabel in dizzy trance,
Stumbling on the unsteady ground—
Shudder'd aloud, with a hissing sound ;
And Geraldine again turn'd round,
And like a thing, that sought relief,
Full of wonder and full of grief,
She roll'd her large bright eyes divine
Wildly on Sir Leoline.

The maid, alas ! her thoughts are gone,
She nothing sees—no sight but one !

The maid, devoid of guile and sin,
I know not how, in fearful wise
So deeply had she drunken in
That look, those shrunken serpent eyes,
That all her features were resign'd
To this sole image in her mind :
And passively did imitate
That look of dull and treacherous hate.
And thus she stood, in dizzy trance,
Still picturing that look askance,
With forc'd unconscious sympathy
Full before her father's view——
As far as such a look could be,
In eyes so innocent and blue !

But when the trance was o'er, the maid
Paus'd awhile, and inly pray'd,
Then falling at her father's feet,
" By my mother's soul do I entreat

" That thou this woman send away !"
She said ; and more she could not say,
For what she knew she could not tell,
O'er-master'd by the mighty spell.

Why is thy cheek so wan and wild,
Sir Leoline ? Thy only child
Lies at thy feet, thy joy, thy pride,
So fair, so innocent, so mild ;
The same, for whom thy lady died !
O by the pangs of her dear mother
Think thou no evil of thy child !
For her, and thee, and for no other,
She pray'd the moment, ere she died ;
Pray'd that the babe for whom she died,
Might prove her dear lord's joy and pride !
That prayer her deadly pangs beguil'd,
Sir Leoline !

And would'st thou wrong thy only child,

    Her child and thine?

Within the Baron's heart and brain

If thoughts, like these, had any share,

They only swell'd his rage and pain,

And did but work confusion there.

His heart was cleft with pain and rage,

His cheeks they quiver'd, his eyes were wild,

Dishonour'd thus in his old age;

Dishonour'd by his only child,

And all his hospitality

To th' insulted daughter of his friend

By more than woman's jealousy,

Brought thus to a disgraceful end —

He roll'd his eye with stern regard

Upon the gentle minstrel bard,

And said in tones abrupt, austere—

Why, Bracy! dost thou loiter here?

1 bade thee hence! The bard obey'd;
And turning from his own sweet maid,
The aged knight, Sir Leoline,
Led forth the lady Geraldine!

THE CONCLUSION

TO

PART THE SECOND.

A little child, a limber elf,
Singing, dancing to itself,
A fairy thing with red round cheeks
That always finds, and never seeks,
Makes such a vision to the sight
As fills a father's eyes with light;
And pleasures flow in so thick and fast
Upon his heart, that he at last
Must needs express his love's excess
With words of unmeant bitterness.

Perhaps 'tis pretty to force together
Thoughts so all unlike each other ;
To mutter and mock a broken charm,
To dally with wrong that does no harm.
Perhaps 'tis tender too and pretty
At each wild word to feel within,
A sweet recoil of love and pity.
And what, if in a world of sin
(O sorrow and shame should this be true !)
Such giddiness of heart and brain
Comes seldom save from rage and pain,
So talks as it's most used to do.

Kubla Khan:

OR

A VISION IN A DREAM.

FRAGMENT OF KUBLA KHAN.

———

THE following fragment is here published at
the request of a poet of great and deserved
celebrity, and as far as the Author's own opi-
nions are concerned, rather as a psychological
curiosity, than on the ground of any supposed
poetic merits.

In the summer of the year 1797, the Author,
then in ill health, had retired to a lonely farm-
house between Porlock and Linton, on the Ex-
moor confines of Somerset and Devonshire. In

consequence of a slight indisposition, an anodyne
had been prescribed, from the effects of which
he fell asleep in his chair at the moment that he
was reading the following sentence, or words of
the same substance, in " Purchas's Pilgrimage:"
" Here the Khan Kubla commanded a palace
to be built, and a stately garden thereunto.
And thus ten miles of fertile ground were in-
closed with a wall." The author continued for
about three hours in a profound sleep, at least
of the external senses, during which time he
has the most vivid confidence, that he could not
have composed less than from two to three
hundred lines; if that indeed can be called
composition in which all the images rose up
before him as *things*, with a parallel production
of the correspondent expressions, without any
sensation or consciousness of effort. On awaking
he appeared to himself to have a distinct recol-
lection of the whole, and taking his pen, ink,
and paper, instantly and eagerly wrote down
the lines that are here preserved.   At this

moment he was unfortunately called out by a
person on business from Porlock, and detained
by him above an hour, and on his return to his
room, found to his no small surprise and morti-
fication, that though he still retained some vague
and dim recollection of the general purpose of
the vision, yet, with the exception of some eight
or ten scattered lines and images, all the rest
had passed away like the images on the surface
of a stream into which a stone has been cast,
but, alas! without the after restoration of the
latter :

                                Then all the charm
  Is broken—all that phantom-world so fair
  Vanishes, and a thousand circlets spread,
  And each mis-shape the other.   Stay awhile,
  Poor youth! who scarcely dar'st lift up thine eyes—
  The stream will soon renew its smoothness, soon
  The visions will return! And lo, he stays,
  And soon the fragments dim of lovely forms
  Come trembling back, unite, and now once more
  The pool becomes a mirror.

Yet from the still surviving recollections in his

mind, the Author has frequently purposed to finish for himself what had been originally, as it were, given to him. Σαμεϱον αδιον ασω: but the to-morrow is yet to come.

As a contrast to this vision, I have annexed a fragment of a very different character, describing with equal fidelity the dream of pain and disease.

KUBLA KHAN.

―――――

In Xanadu did Kubla Khan
A stately pleasure-dome decree:
Where Alph, the sacred river, ran
Through caverns measureless to man
   Down to a sunless sea.
So twice five miles of fertile ground
With walls and towers were girdled round;

And here were gardens bright with sinuous rills
Where blossom'd many an incense-bearing tree;
And here were forests ancient as the hills,
And folding sunny spots of greenery.

But oh that deep romantic chasm which slanted
Down the green hill athwart a cedarn cover!
A savage place! as holy and inchanted
As e'er beneath a waning moon was haunted
By woman wailing for her demon-lover!   [ing,
And from this chasm, with ceaseless turmoil seeth-
As if this earth in fast thick pants were breathing,
A mighty fountain momently was forced:
Amid whose swift half-intermitted Burst
Huge fragments vaulted like rebounding hail,
Or chaffy grain beneath the thresher's flail:
And mid these dancing rocks at once and ever
It flung up momently the sacred river.

Five miles meandering with a mazy motion
Through wood and dale the sacred river ran,
Then reached the caverns measureless to man,
And sank in tumult to a lifeless ocean :
And 'mid this tumult Kubla heard from far
Ancestral voices prophesying war !

The shadow of the dome of pleasure
Floated midway on the waves ;
Where was heard the mingled measure
From the fountain and the caves.
It was a miracle of rare device,
A sunny pleasure-dome with caves of ice !

A damsel with a dulcimer
In a vision once I saw :
It was an Abyssinian maid
And on her dulcimer she play'd,

Singing of Mount Abora.

Could I revive within me

Her symphony and song,

To such a deep delight 'twould win me,

That with music loud and long,

I would build that dome in air,

That sunny dome! those caves of ice!

And all who heard should see them there,

And all should cry, Beware! Beware!

His flashing eyes, his floating hair!

Weave a circle round him thrice,

And close your eyes with holy dread:

For he on honey-dew hath fed,

And drank the milk of Paradise.

The Pains of Sleep.

THE PAINS OF SLEEP.

Ere on my bed my limbs I lay,
It hath not been my use to pray
With moving lips or bended knees;
But silently, by slow degrees,
My spirit I to Love compose,
In humble Trust mine eye-lids close,

With reverential resignation,
No wish conceived, no thought expressed!
Only a *sense* of supplication,
A sense o'er all my soul imprest
That I am weak, yet not unblest,
Since in me, round me, every where
Eternal Strength and Wisdom are.

But yester-night I pray'd aloud
In anguish and in agony,
Up-starting from the fiendish crowd
Of shapes and thoughts that tortured me:
A lurid light, a trampling throng,
Sense of intolerable wrong,
And whom I scorn'd, those only strong!
Thirst of revenge, the powerless will
Still baffled, and yet burning still!
Desire with loathing strangely mixed
On wild or hateful objects fixed.

Fantastic passions! mad'ning brawl!
And shame and terror over all!
Deeds to be hid which were not hid,
Which all confused I could not know,
Whether I suffered, or I did:
For all seemed guilt, remorse or woe,
My own or others still the same
Life-stifling fear, soul-stifling shame!

So two nights passed: the night's dismay
Sadden'd and stunn'd the coming day.
Sleep, the wide blessing, seemed to me
Distemper's worst calamity.
The third night, when my own loud scream
Had waked me from the fiendish dream,
O'ercome with sufferings strange and wild,
I wept as I had been a child;
And having thus by tears subdued
My anguish to a milder mood,

Such punishments, I said, were due

To natures deepliest stain'd with sin:

For aye entempesting anew

Th'unfathomable hell within

The horror of their deeds to view,

To know and loathe, yet wish and do!

Such griefs with such men well agree,

But wherefore, wherefore fall on me?

To be beloved is all I need,

And whom I love, I love indeed.

London: Printed by W. Bulmer and Co.
Cleveland-row, St. James's.